MARY, QUEEN OF THE ROSARY

By

Ron Dawson

ISBN: 1-4033-2916-8 (e-book)
ISBN: 1-4033-2917-6 (Paperback)
ISBN: 1-4033-2918-4 (Dustjacket)

Library of Congress Control Number: 2002105680

This book is printed on acid free paper.

Printed in the United States of America
Bloomington, IN

1st Books - rev. 07/25/02

This book is dedicated to my wife, Sherry, my son, Chris, my daughter, Michele, my granddaughter, Crystal, and my grandson, Aaron.

To my good friends
fred and Carie
with best wishes.

Ronnie

9-26-02

Introduction

The Rosary is a combination of prayers and meditation dedicated to the life, death, and Resurrection of Jesus. Through His Mother Mary, we honor and glorify God the Father, the Son, and Holy Spirit.

In the following pages you will see how we praise Jesus and Mary through the Rosary. The Rosary is a powerful tool to be used primarily for the salvation of our souls. By saying the prayers of the Our Father, Hail Mary, and the Glory Be to the Father, we renew our Christian faith and beliefs. This manuscript is unique because the reader has

Ron Dawson

pictures, songs, poems, and prayers in which to meditate the mysteries of the Rosary all in one book.

The Blessed Mother has also promised many graces if you say the Rosary daily. Reap and enjoy the many benefits in this book.

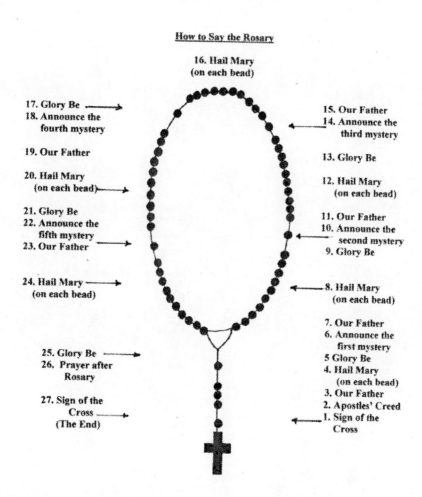

How to Say the Rosary

16. Hail Mary
(on each bead)

17. Glory Be
18. Announce the
    fourth mystery

15. Our Father
14. Announce the
    third mystery

19. Our Father

13. Glory Be

20. Hail Mary
(on each bead)

12. Hail Mary
(on each bead)

21. Glory Be
22. Announce the
    fifth mystery
23. Our Father

11. Our Father
10. Announce the
    second mystery
9. Glory Be

24. Hail Mary
(on each bead)

8. Hail Mary
(on each bead)

7. Our Father
6. Announce the
   first mystery
5 Glory Be
4. Hail Mary
(on each bead)
3. Our Father
2. Apostles' Creed
1. Sign of the
   Cross

25. Glory Be
26. Prayer after
    Rosary

27. Sign of the
    Cross
    (The End)

Image. The Marianist Mission Pamphlet

3

The Rosary is a prayer of five decades of the Hail Mary and each decade is headed by the Our Father and Glory Be to the Father.

The Hail Mary

Hail Mary, full of grace, the Lord is with thee. Blessed art thou among women and blessed is the fruit of thy womb, Jesus. Holy Mary, Mother of God, pray for us sinners, now and at the hour of our death. Amen.

The Our Father

Our Father, Who art in heaven, hallowed be Thy name. Thy kingdom come, Thy will be done, on earth as it is in

Ron Dawson

Heaven. Give us this day our daily bread, and forgive us our trespasses as we forgive those who trespass against us, and deliver us from evil. Amen.

Glory Be To The Father

Glory Be to the Father, Son, and Holy Spirit. As it was in the beginning, is now, and forever shall be, world without end. Amen.

The Apostles' Creed

I believe in God, the Father Almighty, Creator of heaven and earth; and in Jesus Christ, His only Son, Our Lord; who was conceived by the Holy Spirit, born of the Virgin Mary, suffered under Pontius Pilate, was crucified, died and was buried. He descended into hell; the third day He rose again from the dead; He ascended into heaven, sits at the right hand of God, the Father Almighty; from thence He shall come to judge the living and the dead. I believe in the Holy Spirit, the Holy Catholic Church, the communion of the saints, the forgiveness of sins, the resurrection of the body, and life everlasting. Amen.

Ave Maria

By
Walter Scott

"Ave Maria! Maiden mild!
Listen to a maiden's prayer!
Thou canst hear through from the wild,
Thou canst save amid despair.
Safe may we sleep beneath thy care,
Through banished, outcast and reviled.
Maiden, hear a maiden's prayer;
Mother, hear a suppliant child.
   Ave Maria!

Ave Maria! Undefiled!
The flinty couch we must now share
Shall seem with down of ceder piled,
If thy protection hover there.
The murky cavern's heavy air
Shall breathe of balm, if thou has smiled;
Then, Maiden, hear a maiden's prayer;
Mother, list a suppliant child!
   Ave Maria!

Ave Maria! Stainless styled!
Foul demons of the earth and air,
From this their wonted haunt exiled,
Shall flee before thy presence fair.
We bow us to our lot of care,
Beneath thy guidance reconciled;
Hear for a maid a maiden's prayer;
And for a father hear a child.

Ron Dawson

Ave Maria!"

St. Thomas More Series, Prose and Poetry of England
Page 370

After making the sign of the cross we are now ready to mediate on the saying of the Holy Rosary. The Rosary of the Blessed Virgin Mary consists of the following Mysteries:

Joyful Mysteries (5)

1. The Annunciation.
2. The Visitation.
3. The Nativity.
4. The Presentation.
5. The Finding of Jesus in the Temple.

Sorrowful Mysteries (5)

1. The Agony of Jesus in the Garden.
2. The Scourging of Jesus at the Pillar.
3. The Crowning of Jesus with thorns.
4. Jesus carries His cross.
5. The Crucifixion.

Glorious Mysteries(5)

1. The Resurrection of Jesus.
2. The Ascension.
3. The Descent of the Holy Spirit.
4. The Assumption of our Blessed Mother.
5. The Crowning of the Blessed Virgin Mary.

Ron Dawson

The Rosary is a prayer by which we learn to honor the mysteries of the life, passion, death, and glory of Jesus and Mary.

"Ave Maria, gratia plena
Dominus tecum, benedieta tu
In mulierbus et benedictus
Frutus ventris tui Jesus
Sancta Maria, Sancta Maria,
Maria ora pro nobis,
Nobis recatoribus,
Nune et in ora,
In ora mortis nostrae."

(www) avemaria.org/engavemaria:html

"Hail Mary, full of grace
The Lord is with you, blessed are you
Among women and blessed is
The fruit of your womb, Jesus.
Holy Mary, Holy Mary,
Mary pray for us,
Now and at the hour of our death,
Amen."

(www) avemaria.org/engavemaria:html

Ron Dawson

The Virgin

By
William Wordsworth

"Mother! Whose virgin bosom was uncrost
With the least shade of thought to sin allied;
Woman! Above all women glorified,
Our tainted nature's solitary boast;
Purer than foam on central ocean tost;
Brighter than eastern skies at daybreak strewn
With fancied roses, than the unblemished moon
Before her wane begins on heaven's blue coast:
Thy image falls to earth. Yet some. I ween,
Not forgiven, the suppliant knee might bend
As to a visible power, in which did blend
All that was mixed and reconciled in thee
Of a mother's love with maiden purity,
Of high with low, celestial terrene."

St. Thomas More Series, Prose and Poetry of England
Page 361

Ron Dawson

We will now meditate on the Rosary starting with the Joyful Mysteries.

The Annunciation

The Archangel Gabriel was sent by God to call upon a virgin named Mary to inform her that because of her grace with God, she will conceive in her womb, a son, whose name will be called Jesus. The Holy Spirit came upon Mary and she was blessed with child.

The gracious lady was seen by the Archangel Gabriel who tells her "Hail Mary, full of grace."*Luke1,28.* Ever so humble and pious, Mary receives the news with a smile on her beautiful face.

"Blessed and venerable are you, O Virgin Mary, without stain to your virginity you became the Mother of our Savior, O Virgin, Mother of God, He whom the whole

world cannot contain enclosed Himself within your womb, being made man."

Saint Andrews Daily Missal. Page 1037.

Ron Dawson

Sing of Mary, Pure and Lowly

(Hymn)

"Sing of Mary, pure and lowly,
Virgin Mother undefiled,
Sing of God's own Son most holy,
Who became her little child,
Fairest child of fairest mother,
God the Lord who came to earth,
Word made flesh, our very brother,
Takes our nature by his birth.

Sing of Jesus; son of Mary,
In the home at Nazareth,
Toil and labor cannot weary
Love enduring unto death.
Constant was the love he gave her,
Though he went forth from her side,
Forth to preach, and heal, and suffer,
Till on Calvary he died."

Parish Mass Book and Hymnal.
Page 528.

Ron Dawson

The Visitation

Mary calls upon her cousin Elizabeth who is expecting a child of her own soon. Upon greeting Mary, Elizabeth cries, "Blessed art thou among women and blessed is the fruit of thy womb!" *Luke1,92.* Mary helps her cousin with household chores and stays with her for three months.

The Holy Spirit has filled both their hearts with happiness, great joy, and love.
They praise the Heavenly Father for bestowing on them the graces received from above.

"Hail, O Star of ocean,
God's own mother blest.
Ever sinless virgin,
Gate of heavenly rest.

25

Ron Dawson

Taking that sweet Ave,
Which Gabriel came.
Peace confirm
Within us,
Changing Eva's Name

Saint Andrew's Daily Missal.
Page 1040.

Ron Dawson

The Nativity

An edict from Caesar Augustus has Mary and Joseph on their way to Bethlehem. Once there, they find no room for them in any of the inns. At last they find shelter in a hillside stable. Mary brings forth her Son, Jesus. Under the stars, she wraps Him tenderly and lays Him on the straw in the manger.

Angels spread the news of the birth and bring tidings of great joy.
The Lamb of God, Jesus, was born on that Holy Night, to Mary,
Who is the Mother of our Savior and gives birth to a blessed boy.

Shepherds come from all around, along with the Three Wise Men who have followed the great star.

Ron Dawson

All adore the Savior especially the Three Kings who have come from afar.

"Hail Queen of the Heavens!
Hail, Mistress of earth!
Hail, Virgin most pure,
Of Immaculate birth!

Clear Star of the morning,
In beauty enshrined!
O Lady, make speed,
To the help of mankind.

Thee God in the depth
Of eternity chose;
And formed Thee all fair
As His Glorious Spouse;
And called Thee His Word's
Own Mother to be.
By Whom He created
The earth, sky, and Sea."

Our Lady's Book.
Page 77.

Ron Dawson

The Finding of Jesus in the Temple

When Jesus was twelve, Mary and Joseph took Jesus with them to Jerusalem to celebrate the Passover. When the feast was over, Mary and Joseph returned to Nazareth. Jesus remained behind. Mary and Joseph thought Jesus was with the caravan. When they found Him missing they returned to Jerusalem. For three days they searched for him and finally found him in the temple in Israel listening and talking to the priests. Jesus explained to Mary and Joseph that He was doing His Father's business.

O Lord, we pray that we may find Our Son free from harm.

Return Him in your grace and safety that we may have no cause for alarm.

"Hail, Solomon's throne!
Pure ark of the law!
Fair rainbow! And bush,
Which the Patriarch saw.

Hail Gideon's fleece!
Hail blossoming rod!
Samson's sweet honeycomb!
Portal of God!

Well fitting it was,
That a Son so divine
Should preserve from all touch,
Of original sin.

Nor suffer by smallest
Defect to be stained,

35

That Mother, whom He
For Himself, had ordained."

Our Lady's Book.
Page 8.

The Presentation

Mary, Joseph, and Jesus travel to Jerusalem to present Jesus to His Father. Simon meets them in the temple and takes Jesus from Mary. There they sing songs of joy and offer prayers to God the Father.

O Holy Father, behold the immaculate birth,
Of Thy most blessed Son born to Mary here on earth.
They offered prayers and praise in the darkness of the night,
To God we give honor and glory to His infinite light.

"Hail! Virgin most wise!
Hail Deitys shrine!

Ron Dawson

With seven fair pillars,
And Table divine!

Preserved from the guilt
Which hath come on us all!
Exempt, even in the womb,
From the taint of the fall.

O new star of Jacob!
Of Angels, the Queen!
O gate of the Saints!
O mother of men.

O terrible as
An embattled array
Be thou of the faithful
The refuge and stay."

Our Lady's Book. Page 79.

Ron Dawson

The Sorrowful Mysteries

The Agony in the Garden

Jesus takes Peter and James with Him into the inner garden to pray. He tells Peter and James to stay there while He goes deeper into the garden. As Jesus prays, his sweat become drops of blood, for He knows that the time of His death is near.

The Holy Redeemer, all sorrowful and sad, falls to His knees as he prays.

His Precious Blood drips from Him, for His death is near as the bitter passion before Him lays.

"Hail, Israel's King, Hail! David's son confessed!
Who comest in the name of Israel's Lord.

Thy praise in heaven the host angelic sings!
On earth mankind, with all created things.

"Thee once with palms the Jews went forth to meet
Thee now with prayers and holy hymns we greet.

Thee, on Thy way to die, they crowned with praise:
To Thee, now King on high, our song, we raise.

Thee, their poor homage pleased, O gracious King!
Ours too accept, the best that we can bring."

Saint Andrews Daily Missal.
Page 365.

The Scourging of Jesus at the Pillar

Pilate calls together the chief priests and states that he will have Jesus whipped and then let go. Our Lord is led to the pillar, His back is bare. He is tied to the whipping post and the soldiers begin to beat Him. The scourging is finally stopped and Jesus is handed over for crucifixion.

"Hail, Our King, Son of David, Redeemer of the World, whom the prophets have foresaid would come as the Savior of the house of Israel, for the Father sent Thee into the world as a victim for our salvation And all the holy ones from the beginning of the world were waiting Thee and now cry: "Hosanna to the Son of David! Blessed is he that cometh in the name of the Lord!
Hosanna in the highest!"

Saint Andrews Daily Missal.
Page 366.

The Crowning of Jesus with Thorns

Because the Romans knew that Jesus was called a king, they put a robe over Him and gave Him a bench for His throne. The soldiers mock Jesus and proclaim that he must have a crown. They gather a mass of thorns and fashion them into a crown. They then crush the crown into place upon His head. The soldiers then spit on Jesus and mock Him by saying, "Hail, King of the Jews!" *John 19,3.*

See the thorns upon His brow,
How great is His agony now.
Drops of His precious blood are flowing,
Upon His face the great pain is showing.

"Hail, Virginal Mother!
Hail purity's cell!
Fair shrine where the Trinity
Loveth to dwell.

Hail, garden of pleasure!
Celestial balm!
Cedar of chastity,
Martyrdom's palm!

Thou land set apart
From uses profane!
And free from the curses
Which in Adam began

Thou city of God!
Thou gate of the East!
In Thee is all grace,

Ron Dawson

O joy of the blest!"

Our Lady's Book.
Pages 81,82.

Ron Dawson

Jesus Carries His Cross

Pilate condems Jesus to death. The cross is put upon His shoulders. Along the way to Calvary, Jesus stumbles and falls. The soldiers are afraid that Jesus will not make it all the way, they make Simon of Cyrene help Jesus carry His cross. Jesus is tired and weak and falls again. Veronica wipes His face. The women of Jerusalem are weeping as Jesus goes by. Jesus, hurting and stumbling, falls for the third time. He arrives at Calvary where he is stripped of His garments.

The weight of man's sins are upon Him, the sacred time is nigh.
Thus did Jesus carry His cross, crying out to His Father's throne on high.

"Blest Creator of the light,
Making day with radiance bright.

Thou didst o'er the forming earth,
Give the golden light its birth.

Shade of eve with morning ray
Took from Thee the name of day.

Darkness now is drawing nigh;
Listen to our humble cry.

May we ne'er by guilt depressed
Lose the way to endless rest,

Nor with idle thoughts and vain
Bind our souls to earth again.

Rather may we heavenward rise
Where eternal treasure lies;

Purified by grace within
Hating every deed of sin.

Father, what ask be done
Through Thy well-beloved Son;

With the Holy Spirit and Thee Reigning
Through eternity. Amen."

Saint Andrews Daily Missal.
Pages 878,879.

The Crucifixion and Death of Our Lord

The cross is put onto place and Our Lord is cast down upon it. The nails are driven into His hands and feet. He pleads to His Father; "Father, forgive them!" *Luke 24, 33.* The executioners lift the cross and its precious burden aloft and fix it into the rocky socket. Jesus, Our Lord is crucified! He hangs there for three long, agonizing hours. He rewards the good thief's defense of Him with a promise to him that he will see heaven on this day. With His work done, Our Lord gives out a cry, bows His head, and dies.

"On which our Savior's holy side, rent open with a cruel spear of blood and water poured a stream. To wash us from defilement clear.

57

Ron Dawson

O sacred wood! In Thee fulfilled, was holy David's truthful lay!
Which told the world, that from a tree, the Lord showed all nations sway.

Lo, with gall His thirst He quenches: See the thorns upon His brow.
Nails His tender flesh are rending; See His side is opened now.

Honour, blessing everlasting
To the immortal Deity;
To the Father, Son and Holy Spirit Equal praises ever be;
Glory through the earth and heaven
To Trinity in Unity, Amen."

Saint Andrew Daily Missal. Page 883.

Ron Dawson

The Glorious Mysteries
The Resurrection

Easter Sunday is bright and joyous. Our Lord appears first to Mary Magdalene. Mary goes to Our Lord's tomb to anoint His Body but when they get there they find the tomb open and the stone rolled back. An angel appears saying to Mary; "He is not here, but is risen." *Luke 24, 6.*

Our Lord greets the rest of the disciples with the words: "Peace be with you." *John 20,19.* He breathes upon them and gives them the power to forgive the sins of men for whom He has died.

Ron Dawson

"Forth to the paschal Victim, Christians bring
Your sacrifice of praise;
The lamb redeems the sheep,
And Christ the sinless One.
Hath to the Father sinners reconciled,
Together, death and life
In a strange conflict stove.
What thou sawest, Mary, say,
As thou went on the way.
I saw the tomb wherin the living one had lain,
I saw His glory as He rose again;
Napkins and linen cloths, and angels twain:

Yea, Christ is risen, my hope, and He
Will go before you in Galilee.
We know that Christ indeed has risen from the grave:
Hail, Thou King of Victory, Have mercy, Lord, and save."

Saint Andrews Daily Missal.
Page 507.

Ron Dawson

The Glories of the Lord
The King of the Universe

"Sing to the Lord a new song; sing to the Lord, all you lands.

Sing to the Lord; bless his name; announce his salvation, day after day.

Tell his glory among the nations; among all peoples, his wondrous deeds.

For great is the Lord and highly to be praised; awesome is he, beyond all gods. For all the gods of the nations are things of nought, but the Lord made the heavens. Splendor and majesty go before him; praise and grandeur are in his sanctuary. Give to the Lord, you families of nations, give to the Lord glory and praise; give to the Lord the glory due his name! Bring gifts, and enter his courts; worship the Lord in holy attire, Tremble before him, all the earth; say among the nations; The Lord is King. He has made the world firm, not to be moved; he governs the people with equity. Let the heavens be glad and the earth rejoice; let the sea and what fills it resound; let the plains be joyful and all that is in them! Then shall all the trees of the forest exult before the Lord, for he comes; for he comes to rule the earth. He shall rule the world with justice and the peoples with his constancy."

Psalm95.1-13.

The Ascension

Our Lord shows Himself alive to His disciples for forty days and then leads them to Mount Olivet. There He promises that the Holy Spirit will come upon them.

He tells them to witness unto Him, not only in Jerusalem, but to all parts of the world.

A cloud then descends and lifts Him to Heaven. The disciples stand there with mixed emotions gazing up into the heavens where Jesus has gone. Two angels appear and tell the disciples that Jesus has ascended into heaven but shall return.

Ron Dawson

"Ye Men of Galilee, why look you up to heaven? This Jesus who is taken up from you into heaven, shall so come, Alleluia! Lifting up His hands, He blessed them and was carried up to heaven, Alleluia!

Glorify the King of Kings, and sing a hymn to God, Alleluia!
While they looked on, He was raised up and a cloud received Him into heaven, Alleluia!

What wondrous mercy conquered Thee
Our sins upon Thyself to bear.
That quietness dying on the Tree.
Our souls from death's jaw. Thou might'st tear?

Bursting the chaos of the grove,
From captives Thou dost loose their chain;
And conquering death in triumph brave,
Dost at the Father's right hand reign.

Let mercy urge Thee, by Thy grace,
In full our loses to restore;
And granting us to see Thy face,
Enrich us with Thy blest light's store.

Thou guide to heaven, and Thou the way!
Be Thou the goal where our hearts tend.

Be Thou our joy amid tears, we pray.
Be Thou our life's sweet prize and end."

The Saint Andrews Daily Missal.
Pages 569,570.

Ron Dawson

The Descent of the Holy Spirit

The followers of Our Lord, on returning to the Holy City, go back to the upper room where they began to pray. With the apostles are the holy women and Mary, the Mother of Jesus.

Then on Pentecost there is suddenly, the sound as if a mighty wind were coming. Then there appears to them parted tongues, as if they were made of fire and the apostles are filled with the Holy Spirit.

The apostles all begin to speak in different languages which the Holy Spirit had given them to spread the word of Jesus.

"Come, Holy Spirit, send down those beams,
Which sweetly flow in silent streams
From Thy bright Throne above.

O come, Thy Father of the poor,
O come, Thou source of all our store
Come fill our hearts with love.

O Thou of comforters, the best,
O Thou the souls delightful guest,
The pilgrims' sweet relief.
Rest art Thou in our toil, most sweet
Refreshment in the noonday heat,
And solace in our grief."

Saint Andrews Daily Missal. Page 584.

Ron Dawson

Holy Spirit, Lord of Light
(Hymn)

"Holy Spirit, Lord of Light,
From thy clear celestial height,
Thy pure beaming radiance give.
Come, Thou Father of the poor;
Come, with treasures which endure;
Come, Thou Light of all that live.

Thou, of all consolers best.
Thou the souls most welcomed Guest,
Dost refreshing peace bestow,
Thou in toil art comfort sweet;
Pleasant coolness in the heat;
Solace in the midst of woe.

Light immortal, Light divine,
Visit Thou these hearts of Thine,
And our inmost being fill.
If Thou take Thy grace away,
Nothing pure in man will stay;
All his good is turned to ill."

Parish Mass Book and Hymnal.
Page 495.

Ron Dawson

The Assumption of Our Lady.

After all the apostles left, Our Lady went to live with the Apostle John. Her separation from her Son is coming to a close.

All the Apostles are drawn together by a special inspiration to see Mary once more before her death.

After her death and burial, the Apostles go to the tomb where they have laid Christ's Mother. When they open the tomb her body is not there. Joyously they realize that Mary's Son would not permit His Holy Mother's body to see corruption. He has assumed her; as well as her soul, into heaven to be with Him.

Ron Dawson

"Joy to thee, O Queen of Heaven, Alleluia!
He whom thou wast to meet to near. Alleluia!
As He promised, hath risen, Alleluia!
Pray for us to Him thy prayer, Alleluia!

The Saint Andrews Daily Missal.
Pages 913,914.

Ron Dawson

On The Glorious Assumption of Our Blessed Lady
By
Richard Crashaw

"Hark! She is call'd, the parting hour is come;
Take Thy farewell, poor World, Heaven must go home.

A piece of heavenly earth, purer and brighter
Than the chaste stars, whose choice lamps come to light
her,

While through the crystal orbs clearer than they
She climbs and makes a far more Milky Way.

She's call'd! Hark! How the dear immortal Dove
Sighs to his silver mate: "Rise up, my love!"

Rise up, my fair, my spotless one!
The Winter's past, the rain is gone:

The Spring is come, the flowers appear,
No sweets, but thou, are wanting here.

Come away, my love!
Come away, my dove!

Cast off delay;

The court of Heaven is come
To wait upon thee home;

Come, come away!"

Ron Dawson

St Thomas More Series, Prose and Poetry of England.
Page 265.

Ron Dawson

The Crowning of Our Lady as Queen of Heaven

Our Lady is born again, body and soul, into heaven. She is placed on a throne next to her Divine Son and crowned Queen of Angels. From her throne Our Lady offers love and peace to all men. Even as we say her Rosary, she gives us all of God's love.

"Hail, Queen of Heaven enthroned!
Hail by Angels mistress owned!

Root of Jesus, gate of morn,
Whence the world's first true Light was born.

Ron Dawson

"Joy to thee,
Loveleist whom in heaven they see!

Fairest thou where all are free!
Plead with Christ our sins to spare."

Saint Andrews Daily Missal.
Pages 911,912.

"Mary the Dawn; but Christ the perfect Day;
Mary the Gate; but Christ the heavenly Way;
Mary the Root; but Christ the mystic Vine;
Mary the Grape; but Christ the sacred Wine;
Mary the Wheat; but Christ the living Bread;
Mary the Rose-tree; but Christ the Rose Blood-red;
Mary the Fount; but Christ the Cleansing Flood;
Mary the Chalice; Christ the saving Blood;
Mary the Temple; Christ the Temple's Lord;
Mary the Shrine; but Christ its God adored;
Mary the Beacon, Christ the haven's Rest;
Mary the Mirror, Christ the vision Blest."

Our Lady's Book.
Pages 21, 22.

Ron Dawson

Prayer After The Rosary

"Hail! Holy Queen, Mother of Mercy, our life, our sweetness, and our hope.

To you do we cry; poor banished children of Eve. To you do we send up our sighs, mourning and weeping in this valley of tears. Turn then, O most gracious advocate, your eyes of mercy toward us; and after our exile, show us the blessed fruit of your womb, Jesus.

O clement, O loving, O sweet Virgin Mary, Pray for us, O Holy Mother of God. That we may be made worthy of the promise of Christ. O God, whose only-begotten Son, by

Ron Dawson

His life, Death, and Resurrection has purchased for us the rewards of eternal life; grant, we beseech You, that meditating on these mysteries of the most Holy Rosary of the Blessed Virgin Mary, we may imitate what they contain, and obtain what they promise.

Through the same Christ our Lord. Amen."

The Marianist Mission Pamphlet.

Ron Dawson

The Blessed Virgin Mary has appeared to many people over the years in various countries all over the world. Besides her apparitions in Fatima, Portugal and in Lourdes, France; the Virgin Mary has been appearing in Medjugory, (pronounced (Med-u-gory) Yugoslavia since 1981 to present day. She also appears on the anniversary day of Medjugory. Mary has stated in her messages that only through prayer and fasting can wars be stopped. She also states that only through prayer and the saying of her Rosary can we find peace and happiness. We need to be part of God through His Son, Jesus.

91

In Mary's messages she requests the following when praying the Rosary:

1. Pray for peace.
2. Pray for the conversion of sinners.
3. Pray to stop abortions.
4. Pray for the souls in purgatory.
5. Pray for Pope John Paul II.
6. Pray for the special intentions of the Blessed Mother.

Ron Dawson

The Ancient Woman
By
Ron Dawson

The woman in white has appeared to us many times over the years,
She has warned us, the human race, that sins against God have caused her many fears.

The three young children at Fatima were told of the things to come,
The visions warn us of the terrible events that will happen in this world, yet her warnings are only heeded by some.

Ron Dawson

The three prophecies revealed to the three children were of great horror, it makes one shake.
The King's Mother cries as tears fall down her cheeks; is she telling us of Armageddon, or the coming of the great quake?

The Ancient Woman appears to us in hope of redeeming the world, to be better Christians, and that sins against God must cease.
We ask and pray that wars and famine across the globe stop, as Mary, the Mother of God, pleads for peace.

Ron Dawson

Peace
By
Ron Dawson

The Armistice will be signed between the countries bringing about amity.

Peace and love along with order and friendship at last will bring unity.

Put aside your weapons of war.
Work together to overcome sickness and disease. Help your fellow man forevermore.

Ron Dawson

Fight no more in the killing fields of your countries. Mend your differences with brotherhood.
Worship together, giving thanks to God for peace in the world, as people should.

The winds of war shall be gone forever.
Give peace a chance, make it your endeavor.

Ron Dawson

———

Conclusion

Touch the Sacred Heart of Jesus through Mary and her Rosary. Convert others to say the Rosary. Become God's instrument for His glory and receive an abundance of graces for your soul. Use this book in your daily prayer. Pass it on to a friend or a teacher. Teach the children to say it. Preach the devotion of Mary and pray the Rosary. May the peace of the Lord be with you .

Ron Dawson

Bibliography

1. <u>The Marianist Mission Pamphlet</u>. Copyright 1993. The Marianist Mission, Dayton, Ohio. *Image.*

2. Ave Maria. <u>www.*Avemaria.org/engavemaria.html.*</u>

3. <u>The Saint Andrews Daily Missal</u>.Copyright 1961. The E. M. Lohmann Company, Saint Paul, Minnesota. Pages 365, 366, 507, 569, 570, 584, 878, 879, 883, 911, 912, 913, 914, 1037, and 1040.

4. <u>Our Lady's Book</u>. Copyright 1942. Vincentian Foreign Mission Society, St. Louis, Missouri. Pages 8, 21, 77, 79, 81, and 82.

5. <u>St. Thomas More Series, Prose and Poetry of England.</u> Copyright 1955. The L.W. Singer Company, Inc. Syracuse, New York. Pages 265, 361, and 370.

6. <u>Parish Mass Book and Hymnal.</u> Copyright 1965 by Catholic Book Publishing Company, New York. Pages 495 and 528.

Born in Wyandotte, Michigan, in 1939, Ron Dawson was educated at Saint Patrick's High School in Wyandotte, Michigan, the University of Detroit, the North American School of Conservation, the University of Michigan, Wayne County Community College. Ron is currently enrolled in The International Library of Poetry's Laureate Program.

A retired supervisor from the Ford Motor Company in Saline, Michigan, he has had several poems published along with a published book, <u>Practical Poetry</u>. He also has won numerous awards for his poetry.

Married, with two children and two grandchildren, he enjoys writing, hunting, fishing, and golf.

Ron Dawson

ABOUT THE AUTHOR

Born in Wyandotte, Michigan, in 1939, Ron Dawson was educated at Saint Patrick's High School in Wyandotte, Michigan, the University of Detroit, the North American School of Conservation, the University of Michigan, Wayne County Community College. Ron is currently enrolled in The International Library of Poetry's Laureate Program.

A retired supervisor from the Ford Motor Company in Saline, Michigan, he has had several poems published along with a published book, *Practical Poetry*. He also has won numerous awards for his poetry.

Married, with two children and two grandchildren, he enjoys writing, hunting, fishing, and golf.